Tables of Content

B. Understanding your competition

C. Developing a unique value proposition

D. Strategies for standing out from other websites

E. Best practices for maintaining a competitive edge

IV. Website Structure and Technical SEO

A. Overview of website structure and technical SEO

B. Importance of a user-friendly website

C. Key elements of website structure

D. Common technical SEO issues and their impact

E. Tips for improving website structure and technical SEO

F. Best practices for maintaining good website structure and technical SEO

V. Conclusion

A. Recap of the key challenges in SEO

B. Overview of strategies for overcoming these challenges

C. Encouragement to continue learning and improving SEO skills

D. Final thoughts

Chapter 1

Introduction to SEO Basics: Overcoming Key Challenges in Search Engine Optimization

If you're just starting out with SEO, the world of search engine optimization can seem overwhelming and chaotic. With countless algorithms to decipher, confusing terminology to understand, and intense competition to beat, it's no wonder so many people feel intimidated by SEO.

But let us be the first to tell you this: SEO is not as scary as it seems. In fact, once you get a handle on the basics and learn how to overcome the key challenges, you'll find that SEO is a fascinating and rewarding field.

The purpose of this book is to help beginners navigate the world of SEO, with a focus on overcoming the key challenges that are most likely to trip you up. Whether you're a small business owner looking to improve your website's visibility, a blogger trying to reach a wider audience, or a marketer looking to enhance your digital marketing skills, this book is for you.

So why is SEO so important? In today's world, the internet has become the primary source of information for millions of people. When people are searching for products, services, or information online, they turn to search engines like Google, Bing, and Yahoo. And when your website appears at the top of the search engine results, you'll get more traffic, more leads, and more sales.

But with so many websites out there, how do you get your website to stand out? How do you make sure your website appears at the top of the search engine results, ahead of your competition? The answer is SEO.

SEO is the process of optimizing your website to rank higher in the search engine results, and it's a crucial component of any effective digital marketing strategy. But before you can start optimizing your website, you need to understand the key challenges you'll face along the way.

One of the biggest challenges in SEO is keyword research and targeting. Finding the right keywords and phrases to target can be a real headache, and if you don't do it right, you'll be missing out on valuable traffic and leads.

Another major challenge in SEO is competition. There's a lot of competition in search engine rankings, and it can be difficult to stand out among other websites. But with the right strategies and tactics, you can carve out a unique place for yourself in the search engine results and start attracting more traffic, leads, and sales.

Website structure and technical SEO is another big challenge that many beginners face. Issues with website structure, such as broken links, crawl errors, and poor mobile optimization, can seriously impact your search engine rankings and hold you back from reaching your full potential.

Overview of the Book and Its Purpose

Are you tired of feeling lost and overwhelmed in the world of SEO? Do you want to make sure your website is optimized for search engines and ready to attract more traffic, leads, and sales? If so, this book is for you.

The purpose of "SEO Basics: Overcoming Key Challenges in Search Engine Optimization" is to empower beginners with the knowledge and skills they need to succeed in SEO. Our goal is to help you overcome the key challenges that are holding you back and start reaching your full potential.

We know how confusing and overwhelming SEO can be for beginners. With so much information out there, it's hard to know where to start. But don't worry, we've got your back. This book is designed specifically for beginners, with a focus on the most important and relevant aspects of SEO.

In this book, you'll learn about keyword research and targeting, and how to choose the right keywords to optimize your website for search engines. You'll also learn about competition, and how to stand out in the search engine rankings and attract more traffic, leads, and sales.

We'll also cover website structure and technical SEO, and show you how to ensure your website is optimized for both users and search engines. You'll learn about common technical SEO issues, such as broken links and crawl errors, and how to fix them to improve your search engine rankings.

Our aim is to help you overcome the key challenges in SEO and start reaching your full potential. We want to help you gain the confidence and skills you need to succeed in SEO, and to take your website to the next level. Whether you're a small business owner, a blogger, or a marketer, this book is for you.

So don't wait any longer. Start reading "SEO Basics: Overcoming Key Challenges in Search Engine Optimization" today, and start reaching your full potential in SEO. Together, we can help you overcome the key challenges in SEO and start making a real impact online.

With our step-by-step guidance and practical tips, you'll be able to optimize your website for search engines like never before. And you'll be able to experience the thrill of watching your website rise up the search engine rankings, as you attract more and more visitors, leads, and sales.

SEO is not just about ranking higher in the search engine results, it's about reaching the right people at the right time and delivering the right message. By overcoming the key challenges in SEO, you'll be able to connect with your target audience and grow your business.

So don't let the challenges of SEO hold you back any longer. Embrace the opportunities and start taking control of your online presence. With "SEO Basics: Overcoming Key Challenges in Search Engine Optimization," you'll have everything you need to succeed in SEO. So why wait? Start reading today and unleash your full potential in the world of SEO.

Explanation of SEO and Its Importance

Do you feel like your website is lost in the vast ocean of the internet? Do you want to make sure your website is seen by the right people, at the right time? If so, then you need to understand the importance of SEO, or Search Engine Optimization.

SEO is the process of optimizing your website to rank higher in the search engine results, and to reach more people who are searching for the products, services, or information you offer. It's a critical component of your online success, and it can help you connect with your target audience, grow your business, and achieve your goals.

Imagine for a moment, the feeling of frustration and disappointment when you've worked hard to create a website, but no one seems to be visiting it. It's a feeling we've all experienced, but with SEO, you can turn that frustration into excitement and success.

With SEO, you can make sure your website is seen by the right people, at the right time. You can reach potential customers who are searching for what you have to offer, and you can connect with them on a deeper level. You can deliver your message, build your brand, and grow your business, all with the power of SEO.

The importance of SEO goes beyond just traffic and rankings. It's about being found by the right people, at the right time, and delivering the right message. It's about being discovered by potential customers who are looking for what you have to offer, and it's about building trust and credibility with your target audience.

SEO is not just about ranking higher in the search engine results, it's about delivering a better user experience for your visitors. It's about making sure your website is fast, easy to use, and accessible on any device. It's about providing valuable, relevant, and high-quality content that answers your audience's questions and solves their problems.

SEO is a long-term investment in your online success. It's not a one-time thing, it's a continuous process of learning, experimenting, and improving. But the rewards of SEO are well worth the effort, as you'll be able to reach more people, connect with them on a deeper level, and grow your business.

So if you want to experience the thrill of reaching more people, connecting with them, and growing your business, then you need to understand the importance of SEO. With the right knowledge and skills, you can overcome the challenges of SEO and start reaching your full potential online.

So don't wait any longer. Start learning about SEO today, and start making a real impact in the world of search. With the power of SEO, you can make sure your website is seen by the right people, at the right time, and achieve your online goals.

Target audience (Beginners)

When it comes to the world of search engine optimization (SEO), the vast array of information and technical jargon can be overwhelming for beginners. It's easy to feel lost and intimidated when you're just starting out, but that doesn't mean you should give up before you even begin.

Think about why you started down the path of SEO in the first place. Maybe you're a small business owner looking to increase your online visibility and reach more customers. Maybe you're a marketer trying to help your company rank higher in search results. Whatever your reason may be, the excitement and passion you have for the potential of SEO is what drives you forward.

Don't let fear hold you back. You have the potential to be a great SEO expert, and with the right guidance, you'll be able to take your skills to the next level. The journey may be tough, but the rewards are worth it. Imagine the thrill of watching your website's search engine rankings soar, knowing that you made that happen with your own two hands.

As a beginner, you may feel like you're starting from scratch, but that's not necessarily a bad thing. You have the opportunity to learn from the mistakes of others and build a solid foundation for your SEO knowledge. You can approach the process with a fresh perspective and come up with innovative strategies that others may not have thought of.

Don't be afraid to ask for help. There are countless resources available to you, from online forums to SEO consultants. Reach out to others in the industry and don't be afraid to ask questions. The more you learn, the more confident you'll become in your ability to tackle even the most challenging SEO problems.

And remember, SEO is a process, not a destination. You won't see immediate results, but that's okay. Keep pushing forward, keep learning, and keep experimenting. With time and patience, you'll start to see the fruits of your labor. The thrill of watching your website climb the search engine rankings is a feeling like no other.

So to all the beginners out there, don't give up. Embrace the challenge of SEO and let your passion drive you forward. With determination and the right guidance, you'll be able to master the art of search engine optimization and achieve the results you're looking for. The journey may be tough, but the rewards are worth it.

As a beginner, it can be tempting to try to tackle every aspect of SEO all at once. However, this approach is often a recipe for burnout. Instead, focus on one area at a time, and make sure you fully understand the concepts and strategies involved before moving on to the next.

One important area to focus on is keyword research and targeting. Keywords are the foundation of any successful SEO strategy, and it's important to take the time to understand how to select and target the right keywords for your website. This may seem like a tedious task, but the rewards are worth it. By targeting the right keywords, you'll be able to drive more relevant traffic to your website, which will help to increase your search engine rankings and visibility.

Another area to focus on is website structure and technical SEO. Your website's structure and the technical elements behind the scenes play a crucial role in your search engine rankings. Common technical SEO issues, such as broken links and crawl errors, can have a negative impact on your rankings and user experience. Make sure you understand the basics of website structure and technical SEO, and take the time to address any issues that may be affecting your website's performance.

Lastly, it's important to understand the competition in search engine rankings. There will always be competition in the world of SEO, but that doesn't mean you can't stand out from the crowd. Take the time to understand your competition, and focus on developing a unique value proposition that sets you apart from others.

In conclusion, as a beginner in the world of SEO, it's important to approach the process with patience and determination. Don't be afraid to ask for help, and don't try to tackle everything all at once. Focus on one area at a time, and make sure you fully understand the concepts and strategies involved. With time and effort, you'll be able to master the art of SEO and achieve the results you're looking for. So don't give up, embrace the challenge, and let your passion for SEO drive you forward.

Chapter 2

Keyword Research and Targeting: The Heart of Search Engine Optimization

The very first step to a successful search engine optimization (SEO) strategy is understanding the power of keywords. Keywords are the lifeblood of your website, the pulse that drives traffic to your pages and propels your content to the top of search engine results pages.

But with billions of websites vying for the same keywords, finding the right phrases to target can feel like an overwhelming and emotional rollercoaster. You pour your heart and soul into creating the perfect content, only to see it buried on page 50 of Google's search results.

But don't give up hope just yet. Keyword research and targeting is a vital component of any successful SEO strategy, and with a little bit of effort, you can uncover the keywords that will unlock the full potential of your website.

The first step to keyword research is understanding your audience. Who are you trying to reach? What are their interests, needs, and desires? Answering these questions will help you uncover the keywords and phrases that will connect with your target audience.

Next, start with a brainstorming session. Write down every keyword and phrase that comes to mind, no matter how seemingly unrelated. Then, use keyword research tools like Google AdWords Keyword Planner or SEMrush to find keywords related to your business, industry, or niche.

When selecting keywords, aim for a balance between popularity and competition. Popular keywords may drive lots of traffic, but they are also highly competitive, making it difficult for your website to rank for those phrases. On the other hand, less popular keywords may be easier to rank for, but they may also drive less traffic.

To find the sweet spot, prioritize keywords with high search volume and low competition. Use tools like the Keyword Difficulty Score in SEMrush to determine the competitiveness of specific keywords.

Once you have a solid list of keywords, it's time to target them. This means incorporating your keywords into your content, meta tags, and website structure. Make sure to use your keywords naturally and in a way that adds value to your content. Keyword stuffing, or overusing keywords, can actually harm your rankings and turn off your audience.

And remember, your keywords are just the beginning. Continuously monitor your website's performance and adjust your keyword strategy as needed. Stay up-to-date on industry trends and changes to search engine algorithms, and continually refine your approach to keyword research and targeting.

Keyword research and targeting may seem like a daunting task, but the payoff is well worth the effort. By finding the right keywords and incorporating them into your SEO strategy, you can unlock the full potential of your website and connect with your target audience in a meaningful and emotional way. So take a deep breath, dive in, and let the magic of keywords take your website to new heights.

One of the most important aspects of keyword research and targeting is to understand the intent behind each search query. This means taking into consideration the motivation behind the searcher and what they are looking to accomplish with their search. Are they looking for information, ready to make a purchase, or seeking out a specific product or service?

By understanding the intent behind each search query, you can tailor your content and target the right keywords that will attract the right audience to your website. For example, if your website offers a specific product or service, you'll want to target keywords that reflect the purchase intent of the searcher, such as "buy X product" or "best X service near me."

Another critical component of keyword research and targeting is to stay up-to-date with industry trends and changes in search algorithms. Search engines are constantly evolving and adjusting their algorithms to provide the best results for users. This means that keywords that were once popular and effective may no longer be as relevant.

By staying informed and adapting your keyword strategy accordingly, you can ensure that your website remains at the forefront of search engine rankings and continues to connect with your target audience.

Finally, keyword research and targeting is not a one-time effort. Continuously monitoring and adjusting your keyword strategy is key to staying ahead of the competition and maintaining a strong presence in search engine results pages. This includes regularly analyzing your website's performance, conducting new keyword research, and updating your content to reflect current trends and industry changes.

In conclusion, keyword research and targeting is the foundation of a successful SEO strategy. It requires effort, attention to detail, and a commitment to ongoing learning and improvement. But with the right approach, you can uncover the keywords that will connect your website with the right audience and take your content to the top of search engine results pages. So embrace the journey, and let the power of keywords work its magic.

Understanding the importance of keywords

Keywords are the lifeblood of any successful SEO campaign. They are the words and phrases that people use to search for information, products, and services online. And they are the key to unlocking the hidden potential of your website, by connecting you with the right audience, at the right time.

Imagine a world where your website is invisible to potential customers. Where your products and services are buried deep beneath a sea of irrelevant content, never to be seen or discovered. That's the reality of the internet if you ignore the power of keywords.

But when you choose the right keywords and incorporate them into your website, you ignite a chain reaction of benefits that can transform your online presence. You tap into the collective desires, needs, and wants of your target audience, and you give them a reason to find and engage with your website.

The process of keyword research is like mining for gold. You sift through vast amounts of data, using advanced tools and techniques, to find the precious nuggets of information that will guide your SEO strategy.

It's a process that requires patience, persistence, and a deep understanding of your target audience. But when you get it right, you unleash a torrent of organic traffic to your website, driving leads, sales, and conversions like never before.

And that's just the beginning. By focusing on keywords, you also improve the user experience of your website. You create content that is relevant, useful, and engaging, making it easier for people to find what they're looking for, and encouraging them to stay longer and explore more.

The impact of keywords can be felt throughout your entire website, from the content on your pages, to the structure and layout of your site. And when you get it right, your website becomes a beacon of information and inspiration, drawing people in with its relevance and authority.

So, if you're looking to boost your online visibility, attract more visitors, and generate more leads and sales, it's time to start thinking seriously about keywords. Because they are the gateway to a world of unlimited potential, where your website becomes a powerful tool for growth and success.

In conclusion, keywords are more than just words and phrases. They are the life force of your website, and the key to unlocking its full potential. By choosing the right keywords and incorporating them into your SEO strategy, you can reach new heights of online success, connecting with the right audience, at the right time, and driving leads, sales, and conversions like never before.

How to conduct keyword research

Keyword research is the foundation of any successful SEO strategy. It's the process of discovering what keywords and phrases people are searching for online and how to best target those terms in your website's content and structure. Conducting keyword research is a thrilling and exciting journey that can uncover new and innovative ways to drive traffic to your website.

Imagine being able to unlock the door to endless streams of targeted traffic with just a few key phrases. The feeling of seeing your website soar to the top of search engine rankings is indescribable, and the thrill of attracting hordes of visitors to your website is simply electrifying.

So, how exactly do you conduct keyword research? It all starts with a deep understanding of your target audience and what they're searching for online. This involves creating a list of potential keywords and phrases, analyzing their search volume, and evaluating their competition level.

One effective way to start is by brainstorming a list of potential keywords related to your business or website. Think about the products or services you offer, what problems you solve for your customers, and what questions they might have about your industry. Write down anything and everything that comes to mind, no matter how obscure it may seem.

Next, use keyword research tools such as Google Keyword Planner, SEMrush, or Ahrefs to evaluate the search volume and competition level of each keyword. These tools will give you an idea of how often each keyword is being searched for and how many other websites are targeting the same keyword. It's important to target keywords with a healthy balance of search volume and low competition, as this will increase your chances of ranking well in search engine results.

Once you've narrowed down your list of keywords, you can start incorporating them into your website's content and structure. This includes using them in your page titles, headings, meta descriptions, and throughout your content.

However, it's important to use keywords in a natural and organic way, as overusing keywords can result in penalties from search engines.

For example, let's say you run a yoga studio. Some keywords to target could be "yoga classes", "best yoga studio", "beginner yoga classes", "yoga teacher training", etc. You can use these keywords in your page titles, such as "Join the Best Yoga Studio for Beginner Yoga Classes" or "Become a Yoga Teacher with Our Yoga Teacher Training Program".

It's also important to continually evaluate and adjust your keyword strategy, as search trends and consumer behavior can change over time. This means regularly analyzing your website's performance and making tweaks to your keyword targeting strategy as needed.

In conclusion, keyword research is a crucial aspect of SEO that can make or break your online success. By understanding your target audience, conducting thorough research, and continuously monitoring and adjusting your strategy, you can unlock the door to endless streams of targeted traffic and achieve the thrill of seeing your website soar to the top of search engine rankings.

Keyword selection tips for beginners

Keyword selection is a crucial aspect of search engine optimization (SEO) that can often be overwhelming for beginners. It is a complex process that involves understanding your audience, researching your competition, and finding the right balance between search volume and competition level. However, by following these tips, you can simplify the process and start targeting the right keywords for your website.

Understand your audience: Before you start researching keywords, you need to understand who your audience is and what they are looking for. Ask yourself questions such as: What is the main purpose of my website? Who is my target audience? What are their pain points and goals? What types of content do they enjoy? Once you have a clear understanding of your audience, you can start researching keywords that are relevant to their needs and interests.

Use keyword research tools: There are many free and paid keyword research tools available that can help you find keywords that are relevant to your website. Some popular tools include Google Keyword Planner, Ahrefs, and SEMrush. By using these tools, you can find keywords with high search volume and low competition, which are ideal for beginners.

Think like your audience: When choosing keywords, it's important to think like your target audience. Try to put yourself in their shoes and imagine what they would search for when looking for information related to your website. For example, if you have a website about healthy eating, your audience may search for keywords such as "healthy recipes," "nutrition tips," or "diet plans."

Consider long-tail keywords: Long-tail keywords are longer phrases that are more specific and targeted. They tend to have lower competition and can drive highly targeted traffic to your website. For example, instead of targeting the keyword "fitness," you could target the long-tail keyword "at-home workouts for beginners."

Check keyword competition: Before you start targeting a keyword, it's important to check the level of competition for that keyword. You can do this by using keyword research tools or by searching for the keyword on Google and seeing how many results are returned. If there are millions of results, it may be difficult to rank for that keyword, especially as a beginner. On the other hand, if there are only a few results, it may indicate that the keyword is not very popular or relevant.

Focus on relevant keywords: When selecting keywords, it's important to focus on relevance. Don't choose keywords that are not related to your website, just because they have high search volume. This will not only result in poor rankings, but it will also provide a poor user experience for your audience. Make sure to choose keywords that are relevant to your website and that provide value to your audience.

Optimize your content: Once you have selected your keywords, it's important to optimize your content for those keywords. This means including the keywords in your title tags, meta descriptions, headings, and throughout the body of your content. However, be careful not to over-optimize your content, as this can result in penalties from search engines.

In conclusion, keyword selection is an important aspect of SEO that can be overwhelming for beginners. However, by understanding your audience, using keyword research tools, thinking like your audience, considering long-tail keywords, checking keyword competition, focusing on relevant keywords, and optimizing your content, you can simplify the process and start targeting the right keywords for your website.

Remember, keyword selection is not a one-time process. As your website grows and your audience changes, you may need to adjust your keywords. Stay focused on providing value to your audience and creating high-quality, relevant content, and the right keywords will come naturally

Keyword targeting strategies

Keyword targeting is one of the most important components of search engine optimization (SEO). The right keywords can drive targeted traffic to your website, increase your visibility in search engines, and ultimately help you achieve your business goals. However, finding the right keywords and phrases to target can be a challenge, especially for beginners. In this article, we will explore various keyword targeting strategies that can help you get started.

Start with broad keywords: Begin by targeting broad keywords that are relevant to your business. For example, if you sell organic skincare products, start with keywords like "organic skincare", "natural skincare", and "green beauty". These broad keywords will give you a good starting point for your keyword research.

Narrow down to long-tail keywords: Once you have a list of broad keywords, you can start narrowing down to more specific long-tail keywords. For example, "organic skincare for sensitive skin", "natural skincare for acne-prone skin", and "green beauty products for mature skin". Long-tail keywords are more specific, and often have less competition, making them a great option for beginners.

Use keyword tools: There are several keyword tools available that can help you with your keyword research. These tools will give you insight into the search volume and competition for various keywords, making it easier for you to make informed decisions about which keywords to target. Some popular keyword tools include Google Keyword Planner, SEMrush, and Ahrefs.

Focus on local keywords: If you are a local business, it is important to focus on local keywords. For example, "organic skincare in Los Angeles", "natural skincare in San Francisco", and "green beauty products in New York". These local keywords will help you reach your target audience in your local area, and increase your chances of appearing in local search results.

Consider your audience's search intent: It is important to consider the search intent behind each keyword. For example, someone searching for "organic skincare products" may be looking for information about the benefits of organic skincare, while someone searching for "buy organic skincare" is looking to make a purchase. By targeting keywords that match your audience's search intent, you can improve your chances of appearing in relevant search results and attracting targeted traffic to your website.

Monitor your rankings: Once you have started targeting specific keywords, it is important to monitor your rankings in search engines. You can use keyword tracking tools to monitor your rankings and see how your website is performing for each keyword. This will help you identify any issues and make adjustments to your keyword targeting strategy as needed.

In conclusion, keyword targeting is an important component of SEO, and can have a significant impact on your website's visibility and success. By following these strategies, you can find the right keywords to target, reach your target audience, and achieve your business goals. Just imagine the thrill of seeing your website appear on the first page of Google search results, or the excitement of hearing from new customers who found you through search engines. With the right keyword targeting strategy, you can make these visions a reality.

Common Mistakes to Avoid in Keyword Research

When it comes to SEO, keyword research is a crucial step that can make or break your online success. The right keywords can drive traffic to your website, boost your rankings, and help you reach your target audience. On the other hand, if you don't conduct keyword research properly, you can end up wasting time, money, and effort on keywords that won't bring you any results.

In this article, we'll highlight some of the most common mistakes to avoid in keyword research so that you can make the most of this critical step in your SEO journey.

Mistake #1: Failing to Conduct Proper Keyword Research

One of the biggest mistakes you can make in keyword research is not doing it at all. Too often, website owners and marketers dive into creating content without taking the time to conduct proper keyword research. This can result in a lack of focus and direction, causing your website to wander aimlessly in the digital wilderness.

The result is a website that struggles to rank, doesn't receive any traffic, and fails to achieve its desired outcomes. To avoid this mistake, take the time to conduct thorough keyword research before you start creating content. This will ensure that your website is focused, well-targeted, and poised for success.

Mistake #2: Not Understanding Your Target Audience

Another common mistake in keyword research is not understanding your target audience. When conducting keyword research, it's essential to know who your target audience is, what they're searching for, and what keywords they're using to find what they're looking for.

If you don't understand your target audience, you're likely to choose the wrong keywords, which will result in a lack of traffic and poor search engine rankings. To avoid this mistake, take the time to get to know your target audience, understand their needs and preferences, and choose keywords that will resonate with them.

Mistake #3: Choosing the Wrong Keywords

Choosing the wrong keywords can be one of the biggest mistakes you can make in keyword research. If you choose keywords that are too broad, too competitive, or too niche, you're likely to see little to no results.

For example, if you're a small business selling handmade soap, choosing the keyword "soap" is likely to be too broad and competitive. On the other hand, choosing a keyword like "handmade soap for sensitive skin" is more targeted and has a better chance of success.

Mistake #4: Ignoring Long-Tail Keywords

Long-tail keywords are longer phrases that are more specific and less competitive than broad, general keywords. They may not receive as much traffic as broad keywords, but they're more likely to bring you qualified traffic and convert into sales.

Too often, website owners and marketers overlook long-tail keywords in favor of broad, general keywords. This can result in a lack of traffic, poor search engine rankings, and a lack of conversions. To avoid this mistake, make sure to include long-tail keywords in your keyword research and target them in your content.

Mistake #5: Not Keeping Up with Changes in Keyword Trends

Keyword trends change over time, and it's essential to keep up with these changes if you want to remain competitive and successful. Failing to keep up with keyword trends can result in a lack of traffic, poor search engine rankings, and a lack of conversions.

For example, if you're a small business selling handmade soap, and you're targeting the keyword "handmade soap," you may find that this keyword is no longer relevant or that there's a new trend emerging that you're not aware of. To avoid this mistake,make sure to regularly monitor keyword trends and adjust your strategy accordingly. Use keyword research tools, such as Google Keyword

Planner, to stay on top of changes and ensure that your website remains relevant and competitive.

Mistake #6: Not Tracking Your Results

The final mistake to avoid in keyword research is not tracking your results. Without tracking your results, you won't know which keywords are working and which are not, making it difficult to make informed decisions about your SEO strategy.

To avoid this mistake, use a tracking tool, such as Google Analytics, to monitor your keyword rankings, traffic, and conversions. This will allow you to see which keywords are driving results, adjust your strategy accordingly, and continuously improve your SEO efforts.

Keyword research is a critical step in SEO, and it's essential to avoid common mistakes in order to see the best results. By understanding your target audience, choosing the right keywords, targeting long-tail keywords, keeping up with changes in keyword trends, and tracking your results, you can ensure that your website is focused, well-targeted, and poised for success.

Don't let these common mistakes hold you back from reaching your SEO goals. Take the time to conduct proper keyword research and make the most of this critical step in your SEO journey.

Chapter 3

Competition

Competition in search engine rankings can feel like an endless battle. With millions of websites vying for a top spot, it can be daunting to even think about trying to stand out from the crowd. The feeling of defeat is all too familiar, as you pour countless hours into keyword research and optimization, only to see your website buried on page 10 of the search engine results. But it doesn't have to be this way. With the right strategies and a bit of determination, you can rise to the top and beat the competition.

The first step to conquering the competition is to understand it. Who are your competitors? What are they doing to rank higher than you? What do they offer that you don't? These are important questions to ask, as the answers will help you to develop a unique value proposition and stand out from the crowd.

Think about it like this: when you're in a crowded marketplace, selling the same product as everyone else, you have to find a way to stand out. Maybe you offer a better price, a better warranty, or a better overall customer experience. The same is true for search engine rankings. You have to find a way to offer something that no one else does.

Here are a few examples of companies that have successfully stood out from the competition:

Airbnb: When they first launched, there were already a number of hotel booking websites on the market. But Airbnb offered something unique: the ability to stay in someone's home, rather than a sterile hotel room. This gave them a unique value proposition and helped them to rise to the top of their industry.

Uber: In a crowded market of taxi and ride-hailing services, Uber differentiated themselves by offering a premium experience. They offer a sleek app, professional drivers, and a more comfortable ride. This set them apart from their competitors and helped them to become a leader in the industry

Apple: Apple has always been known for their innovative products and user-friendly design. In a crowded market of tech companies, they stand out by offering a premium experience that is unmatched by their competitors.

These are just a few examples of companies that have successfully stood out from the competition. But how can you apply these principles to your own website? How can you find a unique value proposition that will help you to rise to the top of the search engine rankings? The answer lies in understanding your competition and developing a strategy that sets you apart.

In this chapter, we'll dive deep into the world of competition in search engine rankings. We'll explore the strategies and techniques you can use to understand your competition and stand out from the crowd. We'll cover everything from conducting competitor research to developing a unique value proposition to implementing effective tactics for maintaining a competitive edge. By the end of this chapter, you'll have the tools and knowledge you need to conquer the competition and rise to the top of the search engine rankings.

Overview of competition in search engine rankings

Competition in search engine rankings can be a fierce and daunting challenge for any website owner. The thought of competing against countless other websites for the same coveted top spots on search engines like Google can feel overwhelming and even disheartening. The reality is that there are only a limited number of first-page search engine results, and there are countless websites vying for those spots. The competition is real, and it's intense.

But competition in search engine rankings can also be seen as a positive thing. It's a sign that there is a high demand for the keywords and phrases you're targeting. This means that there is an opportunity to reach a large audience and potentially drive significant traffic to your website. With the right strategies in place, you can rise above the competition and claim your place at the top of the search engine rankings.

One of the most important steps in competing in search engine rankings is to understand your competition. Take some time to research other websites that are ranking well for the same keywords and phrases that you're targeting. Take note of their strengths and weaknesses and determine what sets them apart from other websites. Understanding your competition will help you identify areas where you can differentiate yourself and stand out from the crowd.

One strategy for standing out from other websites is to develop a unique value proposition. This is a clear and compelling statement that explains what sets your website apart from others and why visitors should choose your website over others. A unique value proposition should be based on a thorough understanding of your target audience and their needs, as well as your own strengths and areas of expertise.

Another strategy for standing out from other websites is to create high-quality, original content. Content is the backbone of any website, and it's what search engines like Google use to determine the relevance and quality of your website. The more relevant and high-quality your content is, the more likely it is to rank well in search engine results. When creating content, focus on addressing the needs and interests of your target audience and use keywords and phrases that are relevant to your niche.

It's also important to focus on website structure and technical SEO. Issues with website structure, such as broken links, crawl errors, and poor mobile optimization, can negatively impact search engine rankings. To improve website structure and technical SEO, make sure your website is easy to navigate, fast-loading, and optimized for mobile devices.

One of the best ways to maintain a competitive edge in search engine rankings is to stay up-to-date with the latest search engine algorithms and best practices. Search engines like Google regularly update their algorithms, and it's important to adjust your SEO strategies accordingly. Stay informed about the latest trends and updates in the world of SEO, and make sure your website is always in compliance with search engine guidelines.

In conclusion, competition in search engine rankings can be intimidating, but it can also be seen as a positive opportunity. To rise above the competition, it's important to understand your competition, develop a unique value proposition, create high-quality content, focus on website structure and technical SEO, and stay up-to-date with the latest search engine algorithms and best practices. With the right strategies in place, you can claim your place at the top of the search engine rankings and drive significant traffic to your website.

Understanding your competition

Understanding your competition is a crucial aspect of search engine optimization (SEO) that can make or break your online success. The idea of having to compete with others for attention and visibility can be overwhelming, but it's also what drives innovation and progress. Knowing who your competitors are and what they're doing can help you develop effective strategies and make informed decisions.

When it comes to SEO, competition refers to other websites that are targeting the same keywords and phrases as you are. The more competition there is for a keyword, the more difficult it will be to rank highly for that term. But competition isn't just about other websites in your industry. It can come from anywhere - including your own website! That's why it's important to understand your competition in order to stand out in the search engine results pages (SERPs).

One of the most effective ways to understand your competition is to analyze their websites. Start by looking at their structure, content, and keywords. What do they do well? What could they improve? This can give you a clear understanding of their strengths and weaknesses and help you identify areas where you can differentiate yourself.

It's also important to look at their backlink profiles. A backlink is a link from one website to another. The more high-quality links a website has, the more authoritative and trustworthy it will appear to search engines. Use tools like Ahrefs, Moz, and Majestic to see who is linking to your competitors and what types of links they have. This information can help you determine the types of links you should be targeting and the strategies you should be using to get them.

Another way to understand your competition is to monitor their rankings. Use tools like Google Analytics, SEMrush, and Moz to track your competitors' rankings for the keywords you're targeting. This will give you a good idea of how well they're doing and what changes you need to make in order to improve your own rankings.

It's also important to understand your competition in terms of audience. Who are they targeting? What are their goals and objectives? This information can help you identify areas where you can differentiate yourself and create a unique value proposition that sets you apart from your competitors.

One of the most important things to remember when analyzing your competition is to stay focused on your own website and goals. Don't let your competitors' success or failure dictate your own. Instead, use the information you gather to make informed decisions and develop effective strategies that will help you achieve your own online success.

For example, if your competitors have a strong presence on social media, it might be time for you to invest in social media marketing. If they're ranking well for specific keywords, it might be time to focus your attention on those terms. If they're offering unique services or products, it might be time to consider doing the same.

It's important to remember that competition can be a good thing. It can drive innovation, encourage growth, and help you stay focused on your goals. But it can also be overwhelming and frustrating. By understanding your competition, you can develop effective strategies, make informed decisions, and ultimately achieve online success.

In conclusion, understanding your competition is a crucial aspect of SEO that can help you stand out in the search engine results pages and achieve online success. It's important to analyze their websites, monitor their rankings, and understand their audience in order to make informed decisions and develop effective strategies. Stay focused on your own website and goals, and remember that competition can drive innovation and encourage growth.

Developing a Unique Value Proposition: Standing Out in a Crowded Online World

In the world of search engine optimization, competition is fierce. With millions of websites vying for top search engine rankings, it can be tough to stand out and capture the attention of your target audience. However, by developing a unique value proposition, you can set yourself apart from the crowd and attract the right people to your website.

A unique value proposition (UVP) is a statement that defines what makes your business, product, or service different from others in your market. It's a powerful tool for differentiating yourself from your competitors and highlighting the benefits and qualities that set you apart. When you have a compelling UVP, you can grab the attention of your target audience, create an emotional connection, and drive more traffic to your website.

So, how do you develop a UVP that makes a real impact? First, it's important to understand your target audience and what they want and need from your business. What are their pain points? What are their goals and aspirations? What sets your business apart from others in your market? Once you have a clear understanding of your target audience, you can begin to craft a UVP that speaks directly to them.

Your UVP should be short, simple, and memorable. It should evoke an emotional response and make your target audience feel something. For example, consider the UVP of the outdoor clothing brand Patagonia: "We're in business to save our home planet." This statement speaks to the values of the brand and creates an emotional connection with customers who are passionate about environmental conservation.

Another example is the UVP of the beauty brand Glossier: "Skin first, makeup second, smile always." This statement captures the brand's approach to beauty and creates an emotional connection with customers who want to look and feel their best.

To develop a UVP that resonates with your target audience, try using vivid, descriptive language that appeals to their emotions. For example, instead of simply saying that your product is "better" or "faster" than others in your market, try using language that creates an emotional connection. For example, you might say that your product "gives you the freedom to live life on your own terms" or "brings joy and happiness to your life."

It's also important to be honest and authentic in your UVP. Don't make false promises or exaggerate the benefits of your business. Your UVP should reflect the true values and goals of your business and speak to the needs of your target audience.

In conclusion, developing a unique value proposition is a crucial step in standing out in a crowded online world. By understanding your target audience and crafting a UVP that speaks directly to their needs and emotions, you can create an emotional connection with your audience and drive more traffic to your website. Remember, your UVP should be short, simple, memorable, and honest. So, take the time to craft a UVP that sets you apart from your competition and captures the attention of your target audience.

Strategies for Standing Out from Other Websites: How to Win the SEO Battle

When it comes to search engine optimization (SEO), the competition can be fierce. With millions of websites vying for the top spots in Google's search results, it's easy to feel overwhelmed and discouraged. But the truth is, standing out from the crowd is possible with the right strategies and a little bit of creativity.

Here are some tips and tactics for rising above the competition and becoming a leader in your industry:

Know your audience: The first step to standing out from other websites is understanding who your target audience is and what they want. Conduct market research, survey your customers, and analyze your website traffic to gain a deep understanding of your audience's needs, interests, and pain points. This information will inform the content and messaging on your website, making it more relevant and appealing to your target audience.

Create unique and valuable content: The best way to capture your target audience's attention is by offering them something they can't find anywhere else. Create unique, high-quality content that solves their problems, educates them, or entertains them. Whether it's a blog post, infographic, video, or podcast, your content should be well-researched, well-written, and visually appealing.

Make your website visually stunning: People are drawn to websites that are aesthetically pleasing and easy to navigate. Invest in a professional website design that is both beautiful and functional. Make sure your website is mobile-friendly and easy to use, with clear navigation, high-quality images, and intuitive layouts.

Establish yourself as a thought leader: Position yourself as an expert in your industry by writing blog posts, giving presentations, and sharing your knowledge on social media. The more you educate and engage your audience, the more they'll see you as a trusted and valuable resource.

Build a strong community: Encourage engagement and interaction on your website by creating forums, comment sections, and social media accounts. Respond to comments and questions, and build relationships with your audience. The stronger your community, the more likely people are to share your content, recommend your website, and return for more.

Leverage the power of video: Videos are a highly engaging and effective way to connect with your audience. Whether it's a product demonstration, a tutorial, or a promotional video, videos have the power to capture your audience's attention, educate them, and build trust. Make sure your videos are high-quality and optimized for search engines.

Optimize your website for search engines: To stand out from other websites, you need to be easily found by your target audience. Optimize your website for search engines by using keywords in your content, meta descriptions, and headings. Make sure your website is technically sound, with no broken links or crawl errors. The more search engine friendly your website is, the more likely it is to rank higher in search results.

Promote your website: Once your website is up and running, it's time to get the word out. Promote your website on social media, in your email signature, and through online advertising. Collaborate with other websites in your industry and reach out to influencers and thought leaders. The more people know about your website, the more traffic you'll receive.

Measure and adjust: Finally, make sure you're tracking your progress and making adjustments as needed. Use Google Analytics to measure your website traffic, bounce rate, and conversion rates. Identify areas for improvement and adjust your strategies accordingly.

In conclusion, standing out from other websites requires a combination of creativity, hard work, and persistence. But with the right approach, you can rise above the competition and become a leader in your industry. Remember, it's not just about having a beautiful website or creating great content, it's about understanding your audience, establishing yourself as a thought leader, and providing value at every step of the way.

One example of a company that has successfully stood out from the competition is Patagonia, the outdoor clothing and gear company. Patagonia has built a loyal following by focusing on environmental activism and corporate responsibility. Their website is visually stunning, with beautiful photos of outdoor adventures and sustainable products. They also have a strong community, with forums for customers to connect and share their experiences. And, their content is unique and valuable, with blog posts and videos about environmental issues, outdoor adventures, and their products.

Another example is Hubspot, the inbound marketing and sales platform. Hubspot has positioned itself as a thought leader in the marketing industry, with a blog that offers valuable insights, tips, and resources for marketers. They also offer a wealth of educational resources, including webinars, ebooks, and courses, all aimed at helping marketers succeed. And, their website is visually appealing and easy to navigate, making it a breeze for visitors to find what they're looking for.

In conclusion, standing out from other websites is not an easy task, but it's one that's worth the effort. By understanding your audience, creating unique and valuable content, and establishing yourself as a thought leader, you'll be well on your way to becoming a top-ranked website in your industry. So, get creative, work hard, and never give up!

Best practices for maintaining a competitive edge

Best practices for maintaining a competitive edge in search engine optimization are crucial for any website looking to stand out from the crowd and rank higher in search engine results pages (SERPs). Whether you're a small business owner, blogger, or marketing professional, it's essential to understand what it takes to keep your website ahead of the competition in an ever-changing digital landscape.

One of the primary components of maintaining a competitive edge is staying up-to-date with industry trends and changes in search engine algorithms. Google and other search engines regularly update their algorithms, and it's essential to stay informed about these updates and adjust your SEO strategies accordingly. For example, the recent shift towards voice search optimization has changed the way that people search for information online. By understanding these changes and optimizing your website for voice search, you can stay ahead of the curve and maintain a competitive edge.

Another critical aspect of maintaining a competitive edge is keyword research and targeting. The right keywords can make all the difference in attracting visitors to your website, but finding the right keywords can be challenging, especially with the ever-increasing competition. Conducting in-depth keyword research and targeting relevant keywords is crucial to your success in SEO. For example, if you run a bakery, targeting keywords such as "baked goods," "homemade cakes," or "artisan breads" will attract visitors looking for high-quality baked goods.

Website structure and technical SEO are also critical components of maintaining a competitive edge. Your website needs to be user-friendly, fast, and easily navigable, and it should be optimized for both desktop and mobile devices. Issues such as broken links, crawl errors, and poor mobile optimization can negatively impact your search engine rankings, so it's essential to address these issues promptly. For example, implementing responsive design and ensuring that your website loads quickly on all devices will help keep your website ahead of the competition and maintain a competitive edge.

Quality content is also crucial for maintaining a competitive edge. The content on your website should be relevant, engaging, and optimized for search engines. Creating high-quality, keyword-optimized content that provides value to your visitors will help your website stand out from the competition and attract more visitors. For example, if you run a blog about healthy living, creating articles about the benefits of a healthy diet, how to start a workout routine, or how to stay motivated to exercise will attract visitors looking for information on healthy living.

Link building is another essential component of maintaining a competitive edge in SEO. High-quality backlinks from authoritative websites can significantly impact your search engine rankings, so it's essential to focus on building high-quality links. For example, if you run an e-commerce website selling pet products, reaching out to pet-related websites and offering to provide them with valuable content in exchange for a backlink can help you build high-quality links and maintain a competitive edge.

Finally, tracking and analyzing your SEO efforts are crucial for maintaining a competitive edge. Properly tracking and analyzing your SEO efforts will help you understand what's working and what's not, and it will allow you to make informed decisions about your SEO strategies. For example, using tools such as Google Analytics and Google Search Console will give you valuable insights into your website's performance and help you understand how you can improve your SEO efforts to maintain a competitive edge.

In conclusion, maintaining a competitive edge in SEO requires a combination of staying up-to-date with industry trends and changes in search engine algorithms, keyword research and targeting, website structure and technical SEO, quality content, link building, and tracking and analyzing your SEO efforts. By focusing on these key components and utilizing best practices, you can keep your website ahead of the competition and attract more visitors to your website.

Chapter 4

Website Structure and Technical SEO: The Key to Unlocking Your Website's Potential

As a beginner in the world of search engine optimization (SEO), it can be overwhelming to think about all the different factors that impact your website's visibility and rankings. While keyword research and competition analysis are important aspects of SEO, there is one element that is often overlooked but equally crucial: website structure and technical SEO.

Imagine your website as a beautiful and intricate machine. Each component, from the navigation menu to the code that powers your pages, must work together seamlessly to ensure your website runs smoothly and effectively. However, if even one small piece is out of place, the entire machine can break down, leaving your website lost in cyberspace and forgotten by potential customers.

That's where website structure and technical SEO come in. They form the foundation of your website, making sure that every page is easily accessible, that your website is optimized for search engines and users, and that your website is error-free. It's the difference between a well-oiled machine that attracts customers and drives sales, and a rusty and broken machine that never even gets a second glance.

Let's take a closer look at some of the key components of website structure and technical SEO:

Navigation: Your website's navigation menu is the roadmap that guides visitors through your site. A clear and intuitive navigation structure makes it easy for visitors to find what they're looking for, while a confusing and cluttered navigation can drive them away.

URL structure: Your website's URLs should be clear and descriptive, making it easy for both users and search engines to understand what each page is about. For example, instead of a URL like "www.example.com/page123", a better URL structure would be "www.example.com/products/shoes/running-shoes".

Mobile optimization: With more and more people accessing the internet on their smartphones and tablets, it's crucial that your website is optimized for mobile devices. This includes having a responsive design that adjusts to different screen sizes, fast loading times, and easy-to-use navigation on mobile devices.

Page speed: A slow-loading website can drive visitors away and negatively impact your search engine rankings. By optimizing images, using a fast web host, and minimizing the use of heavy code, you can ensure that your website loads quickly and smoothly for all visitors.

Crawl errors: Search engines use "bots" to crawl your website and index its pages. Crawl errors, such as broken links or missing images, can make it difficult for these bots to access and understand your site, leading to lower rankings and decreased visibility.

These are just a few examples of the elements that make up website structure and technical SEO. When all of these elements are in place and working together, your website will perform at its best, attracting more visitors, driving more sales, and establishing your brand as a leader in your industry.

So if you're feeling lost or overwhelmed in your SEO journey, remember that website structure and technical SEO are key pieces of the puzzle. By taking the time to understand these elements and making sure they're in place, you'll set your website on a path to success and unlock its full potential.

Overview of website structure and technical SEO

Website structure and technical SEO are two critical components of search engine optimization that can make or break a website's success in search engine rankings. A website with a well-structured and optimized architecture is like a beautifully crafted building that is not only aesthetically pleasing but also functional and efficient. On the other hand, a website with poor structure and technical optimization is like a poorly constructed building that is plagued with leaks, cracks, and other problems that make it difficult to use.

The structure of a website refers to the way in which its content and pages are organized. A website's structure can greatly impact its search engine visibility and usability. A well-structured website is easy to navigate, and it makes it simple for search engines to understand and index its content. This, in turn, can improve a website's search engine rankings and drive more organic traffic to the site.

However, many websites struggle with poor website structure, which can lead to a variety of technical SEO issues. For example, broken links, crawl errors, and slow page loading times can all negatively impact a website's search engine visibility and user experience. These problems can be frustrating for website owners and users alike, and they can make it difficult for search engines to understand and index a website's content.

Another critical aspect of website structure is mobile optimization. With the increasing use of smartphones and tablets to access the internet, it's essential that websites are optimized for mobile devices. A website that is not optimized for mobile devices can have slow page loading times, and its content can be difficult to view and navigate on small screens. This can negatively impact a website's search engine visibility and user experience, and it can lead to higher bounce rates and lower conversions.

To overcome these challenges, it's essential to have a well-structured and technically optimized website. Here are some tips for improving website structure and technical SEO:

Use a clear and intuitive navigation system: A website's navigation system should be easy to use and understand, making it simple for users and search engines to find the content they're looking for.

Create a sitemap: A sitemap is a map of a website's structure that makes it easy for search engines to understand the content and organization of a site.

Fix broken links: Broken links can lead to poor user experience and negatively impact search engine visibility. Use tools like Google Search Console to identify and fix broken links on your website.

Improve page loading times: Slow page loading times can lead to higher bounce rates and lower conversions. Use tools like Google PageSpeed Insights to identify areas for improvement and optimize your website's performance.

Optimize images: Large or poorly optimized images can slow down a website's page loading times. Optimize images by compressing them and using descriptive file names and alt text.

Make sure your website is mobile-friendly: Use responsive design or a separate mobile website to ensure that your website is optimized for mobile devices.

By taking these steps, you can create a well-structured and technically optimized website that not only looks great but also performs well in search engine rankings. A website with a solid foundation and optimized architecture is like a beautiful building that is both aesthetically pleasing and functional. It provides a great user experience and makes it easy for search engines to understand and index your content, driving more organic traffic and increasing conversions.

In conclusion, website structure and technical SEO are critical components of search engine optimization that can greatly impact a website's success in search engine rankings. By taking the time to optimize these aspects of your website, you can create a beautiful and functional online presence that provides a great user experience and drives more organic traffic to your site.

The Importance of a User-Friendly Website: Why it Matters More Than You Think

A website is the digital storefront of a business. It's the first thing a potential customer sees and the lasting impression they carry with them. A user-friendly website can make all the difference between a customer who clicks away, never to return, or one who becomes a loyal customer. It's essential for businesses to understand the importance of a user-friendly website and the impact it has on their success.

Think about the last time you landed on a website that was cluttered, slow to load, or difficult to navigate. How did you feel? Frustrated? Annoyed? Confused? Chances are, you quickly clicked away, searching for a better option. This is the visceral emotional response that businesses need to understand. A user-friendly website creates a positive emotional response and a sense of trust, while a poorly designed website elicits frustration and mistrust.

A user-friendly website starts with a clean, intuitive design that is easy to navigate. A website should have a clear and concise structure, with logical categories and menus. The use of clear headings and subheadings, bullet points, and images can make it easier for users to find what they're looking for. A website should also load quickly, with no broken links or error pages. A website that is slow to load or constantly crashes will drive visitors away and negatively impact a business's search engine rankings.

A user-friendly website also takes into account the user's device and screen size. In today's digital age, it's essential for a website to be mobile-friendly and responsive. A website that is optimized for mobile devices will ensure that it can be easily accessed and navigated on any device, from a desktop computer to a smartphone. A mobile-friendly website not only improves the user experience, but it also helps businesses rank higher in search engine results, as search engines prefer mobile-friendly websites.

Accessibility is another critical aspect of a user-friendly website. A website should be accessible to all users, including those with disabilities. This means using clear and concise language, providing alt-text for images,and using appropriate font sizes and colors that are easy to read. It's also important to ensure that the website can be navigated using only a keyboard and screen reader, making it accessible to those with visual or motor disabilities.

In addition to design and accessibility, the content of a website is also crucial in creating a user-friendly experience. A website should provide clear, concise, and relevant information, making it easy for users to find what they're looking for. The content should be well-organized and easy to read, with a clear call-to-action for the user. A user-friendly website also includes helpful resources, such as FAQs, customer support, and clear policies.

An excellent example of a user-friendly website is Apple. Their website is clean, intuitive, and easy to navigate, with clear categories and menu options. The website is optimized for mobile devices, with a responsive design that adjusts to different screen sizes. Apple also provides clear and concise information, with a clear call-to-action for customers to purchase their products.

Another great example is Amazon. Their website is user-friendly and optimized for all devices, making it easy for users to search and purchase products. The website is well-organized, with clear categories and menu options, and provides helpful resources, such as customer support and product information.

In conclusion, the importance of a user-friendly website cannot be overstated. A website is the digital storefront of a business, and creating a positive user experience can have a significant impact on a business's success. A user-friendly website starts with a clean and intuitive design, optimized for all devices, with accessible and well-organized content. By taking the time to create a user-friendly website, businesses can build trust and establish a strong online presence.

Key Elements of Website Structure: The Foundation for Search Engine Success

Website structure is the backbone of your online presence. It determines the way search engines interact with your site and the experience users have when they visit. A well-structured website is essential for achieving high search engine rankings and providing a positive user experience.

In this section, we'll delve into the key elements of website structure and why they are so important for search engine optimization (SEO).

URL Structure

Your URL structure is the foundation of your website. It's the first thing search engines see when they crawl your site, so it's essential to make sure it's clear and concise. URLs should be short and descriptive, using keywords that accurately reflect the content on the page.

For example, a URL like "www.example.com/about" is much more meaningful than "www.example.com/pageid=17". The former gives users and search engines a clear idea of what the page is about, while the latter is confusing and unhelpful.

Navigation

Navigation is one of the most critical elements of website structure. It helps users find what they're looking for on your site and gives search engines an idea of the content you have available. Navigation should be clear and intuitive, using descriptive headings and subheadings to guide users through your site.

A website with poor navigation is like a maze – users get lost and frustrated, and search engines struggle to understand the content on your site. A well-structured navigation system, on the other hand, is like a map – users can easily find what they're looking for, and search engines can quickly index your content.

Content

Content is king when it comes to SEO. It's what search engines are looking for when they crawl your site, so it's essential to make sure it's high-quality, relevant, and keyword-optimized. Content should be well-written, easy to read, and provide value to your users.

A website with poor quality content is like a desert – it offers nothing of value to users or search engines. A site with high-quality content, however, is like an oasis – it provides value to users and is easily indexed by search engines.

Headings

Headings are another important element of website structure. They help to organize your content and make it easier for users and search engines to understand the main points of your page. Headings should be descriptive and use relevant keywords, with H1 headings being the most important.

A page with poorly formatted headings is like a jumbled mess – it's confusing and difficult to understand. A page with well-structured headings, on the other hand, is like a well-organized book –

it's easy to understand and provides value to users and search engines.

Alt Text

Alt text is a critical element of website structure for images. It provides a text description of an image and is used by search engines to understand the content on your page. Alt text should be descriptive and include relevant keywords, but avoid over-optimizing and keyword stuffing.

A page with poor alt text is like a picture with no caption – it's missing important information and doesn't provide value to users or search engines. A page with well-written alt text, however, is like a picture with a meaningful caption – it provides value and context to users and search engines.

In conclusion, the key elements of website structure – URL structure, navigation, content, headings, and alt text – are the foundation of a successful website. They help to provide a positive user experience, ensure search engines can easily understand your content, and ultimately drive more traffic and higher search engine rankings.

By focusing on these key elements, you can create a website that is not only visually appealing, but also optimized for search engines. Here are a few tips to keep in mind as you work on your website structure:

Keep URLs short and descriptive

Make sure navigation is clear and intuitive

Create high-quality, keyword-optimized content

Use headings to organize your content

Write descriptive alt text for images

Remember, your website structure is the foundation for search engine success. By focusing on these key elements, you can build a website that is both user-friendly and optimized for search engines. So take the time to get it right, and you'll see the rewards in the form of increased traffic and higher search engine rankings.

Common Technical SEO Issues and Their Impact

As a beginner in the world of SEO, it can be overwhelming to navigate the many different elements and technicalities involved in optimizing your website for search engines. Unfortunately, technical SEO issues can have a devastating impact on your website's rankings, traffic, and overall success. If you're not careful, these issues can sabotage your efforts to achieve a higher search engine ranking and leave you feeling frustrated and defeated.

Broken Links

Broken links are one of the most common technical SEO issues that beginners face. These are links on your website that lead to pages that are no longer available or have been moved. Not only do they create a poor user experience, but they can also harm your website's search engine rankings. Broken links send a signal to search engines that your website is not well-maintained and unreliable, causing them to lower your rankings in search results.

Crawl Errors

Crawl errors occur when search engine crawlers are unable to access certain pages on your website. This can happen for a variety of reasons, such as broken links, incorrectly formatted URLs, or pages that are blocked by robots.txt files. Crawl errors prevent search engines from properly indexing your website and can negatively impact your rankings in search results.

Poor Mobile Optimization

With the increasing number of people accessing the internet through mobile devices, it's crucial to have a mobile-optimized website. If your website is not optimized for mobile devices, you risk losing out on a significant portion of your potential audience. Poor mobile optimization can also harm your website's search engine rankings, as search engines favor websites that provide a good user experience across all devices.

Duplicate Content

Duplicate content is a major issue that can harm your website's search engine rankings. Duplicate content refers to pages on your website that have the same or similar content as other pages. This confuses search engines and makes it difficult for them to determine which page should be ranked higher in search results. As a result, your website's rankings in search results can be impacted, and you may lose out on valuable traffic.

Slow Loading Speed

A slow loading website can be a major turn-off for users, leading them to quickly abandon your site in favor of a faster alternative. Slow loading speed can also negatively impact your website's search engine rankings, as search engines favor websites that provide a fast, seamless user experience.

Inadequate Sitemap and Robots.txt File

A sitemap is a file that lists all the pages on your website, making it easier for search engines to crawl and index your site. A robots.txt file, on the other hand, is used to specify which pages on your site should be crawled and indexed by search engines. If your website does not have a sitemap or has an incorrectly formatted robots.txt file, search engines may struggle to properly crawl and index your site, impacting your website's search engine rankings.

The impact of technical SEO issues can be devastating to your website's search engine rankings and overall success. These issues can prevent search engines from properly crawling and indexing your site, causing your website to be penalized in search results. This can result in a significant decrease in traffic and conversions, leaving you feeling frustrated and defeated in your efforts to achieve a higher search engine ranking.

In conclusion, technical SEO issues are a common challenge that beginners face in optimizing their website for search engines. These issues can have a significant impact on your website's search engine rankings, traffic, and overall success, making it crucial to address and resolve them promptly. By staying vigilant and proactively addressing technical SEO issues, you can ensure that your website is well-optimized and on its way toachieving a higher search engine ranking.

To prevent technical SEO issues, it's important to regularly monitor and audit your website. This involves checking for broken links, crawl errors, and poor mobile optimization, as well as checking for duplicate content and slow loading speed. It's also important to keep your sitemap and robots.txt file up-to-date and correctly formatted to ensure that search engines can properly crawl and index your site.

In addition to regularly monitoring and auditing your website, it's also important to work with a trusted SEO agency or consultant who can provide expert guidance and support in resolving technical SEO issues. They can help you identify and resolve technical SEO issues, and provide recommendations on how to improve your website's overall optimization.

Investing in technical SEO is a crucial step in achieving a higher search engine ranking and driving more traffic and conversions to your website. By addressing common technical SEO issues, you can ensure that your website is well-optimized and on its way to reaching its full potential. So don't let technical SEO issues hold you back – take the steps necessary to resolve them and achieve a higher search engine ranking today.

Tips for Improving Website Structure and Technical SEO

Website structure and technical SEO are the backbone of your website, providing the foundation for your search engine optimization efforts. Neglecting these important elements can lead to serious consequences, including poor search engine rankings, low user engagement, and even lost traffic. If you're struggling with website structure and technical SEO, don't despair. By following a few simple tips, you can improve the health of your website and boost your search engine rankings.

Use a Clean and Well-Organized URL Structure

Your website's URL structure is critical for both users and search engines. It should be clean, easy to read, and intuitive. Use clear and concise URLs that accurately reflect the content of each page. Avoid using numbers and special characters, and keep the structure as simple as possible.

For example, instead of using a URL like this: www.example.com/article?id=1234, use a URL like this: www.example.com/article/title-of-article.

Fix Broken Links

Broken links can be frustrating for users and detrimental to your website's search engine rankings. Regularly check for broken links and fix them promptly. You can use a free online tool like Dead Link Checker to find and fix broken links.

Optimize Your Website for Mobile Devices

More and more people are using mobile devices to access the internet, so it's essential to optimize your website for mobile devices. Make sure your website is responsive, meaning it adjusts its layout to fit the screen size of the device being used. Use large, easy-to-read fonts, and place buttons and links where they're easy to tap.

For example, if you have a restaurant website, your menu should be easy to view and select on a mobile device, without having to zoom in and out.

Use a Sitemap

A sitemap is a map of your website that helps search engines understand the structure of your site and the content it contains. By creating and submitting a sitemap to search engines, you can improve your website's visibility and rankings.

Use Header Tags

Header tags (H1, H2, H3, etc.) help search engines understand the structure and hierarchy of your content. Use H1 tags for the main title of your page, and H2 tags for subheadings. Be careful not to overuse header tags, as this can have a negative impact on your search engine rankings.

Minimize Loading Time

Website loading speed is a critical factor in user experience and search engine rankings. Make sure your website loads quickly by compressing images, using a fast hosting provider, and minimizing the use of large, heavy plugins and scripts.

For example, a website that takes more than 3 seconds to load can experience a significant decrease in user engagement and even result in a high bounce rate, which tells search engines that users aren't finding what they're looking for on your site.

Use Alt Text for Images

Alt text is a text description of an image that is displayed if the image can't be loaded. It's important for both users and search engines. Use descriptive alt text that accurately describes the content of the image. This will help search engines understand the content of your website and improve your search engine rankings.

In conclusion, website structure and technical SEO are essential components of your search engine optimization strategy. By following these tips, you can improve the health of your website and boost your search engine rankings. Don't let website structure and technical SEO be an afterthought, as neglecting these important elements can lead to serious consequences.

Best practices for maintaining good website structure and technical SEO

Website structure and technical SEO are essential components of a successful search engine optimization (SEO) strategy. A well-structured and technically optimized website not only provides a better user experience but also improves search engine rankings and drives organic traffic. Maintaining good website structure and technical SEO can be challenging, but it's worth the effort to achieve long-term success.

A good website structure makes it easier for search engines to crawl and index your website. A well-structured website has a clear hierarchy, easy navigation, and relevant, keyword-optimized content. Technical SEO includes optimizing your website for speed, mobile responsiveness, and security, among other factors. When these elements are in place, you can be confident that your website is ready to compete and succeed in the search engine rankings.

One of the most important best practices for maintaining good website structure is to ensure that your website is easy to navigate. This means having a clear hierarchy of categories and subcategories, making it easy for both users and search engines to understand the content of your website. A simple navigation structure with intuitive categories and subcategories helps to keep your website organized and makes it easy for users to find what they're looking for.

Another important aspect of website structure is having a clear and concise URL structure. URLs should be short, descriptive, and contain relevant keywords. For example, instead of a URL like "www.example.com/page123", a better URL would be "www.example.com/category/subcategory/page-title". This makes it easier for both users and search engines to understand the content of your page.

In addition to a well-structured website, technical SEO is crucial for improving search engine rankings. This includes optimizing your website for speed, mobile responsiveness, and security. A slow website can lead to a high bounce rate, as users won't wait for your website to load. To improve speed, you can optimize images, reduce file sizes, and use a content delivery network (CDN).

Mobile responsiveness is becoming increasingly important, as more and more users are accessing the internet from their mobile devices. A website that isn't mobile-friendly will not only provide a poor user experience but will also be penalized by search engines. To ensure that your website is mobile-responsive, use responsive design and test your website on different devices and screen sizes.

Security is another important aspect of technical SEO. A website that isn't secure can lead to a loss of trust among users and can even result in a security breach. To ensure that your website is secure, use an SSL certificate, keep your website and plugins up-to-date, and implement best practices for password security.

In conclusion, maintaining good website structure and technical SEO is essential for long-term success in the search engine rankings. A well-structured website with a clear hierarchy, easy navigation, and relevant content, along with a fast, mobile-responsive, and secure website, will help to improve your search engine rankings and drive organic traffic. Remember, the small effort you put into maintaining good website structure and technical SEO will pay off in the long run, as it will make your website stand out from the competition and provide a better user experience. Don't wait any longer to take the steps necessary to achieve success with your website – get started today!

Chapter 5

Conclusion

Congratulations, you have reached the end of this book and have taken a significant step towards becoming an expert in SEO. The challenges in search engine optimization can seem overwhelming, but by taking a structured and methodical approach, you can overcome them.

In this book, we have explored the challenges of keyword research and targeting, competition, and website structure and technical SEO. We have discussed the importance of each of these elements and provided strategies for overcoming them.

By now, you have gained a deep understanding of the role that keywords play in SEO and how to choose the right keywords to target. You have also learned about the importance of competition and how to stand out from other websites in search engine rankings. Finally, you have learned about the key elements of website structure and technical SEO, and how to improve these elements to achieve better rankings.

As you continue on your SEO journey, remember that there is always more to learn and that the field of SEO is constantly evolving. Keep up with the latest trends and best practices, and stay curious and inquisitive.

Think about the impact that SEO can have on your website and your business. By improving your rankings, you can reach more people, generate more leads, and ultimately drive more revenue. The impact can be truly transformative.

In conclusion, we encourage you to keep pushing yourself and to never give up on your SEO journey. Remember that the journey is just beginning, and that there are always new challenges to overcome and new skills to master. With determination, patience, and a commitment to continuous learning, you will reach your goals and achieve success in search engine optimization.

Take inspiration from the words of the great philosopher, Lao Tzu: "The journey of a thousand miles begins with one step." By reading this book, you have taken that first step. Now, it's time to keep moving forward, one step at a time, towards your ultimate goal of becoming an SEO expert.

Recap of the Key Challenges in SEO

SEO is a critical aspect of digital marketing that can make or break the success of a website. It requires a combination of technical know-how, creativity, and strategy to achieve high search engine rankings and drive organic traffic to a website. Unfortunately, SEO also presents a number of challenges that can be difficult to overcome, particularly for beginners. In this section, we will recap some of the key challenges in SEO and provide tips for overcoming them.

One of the biggest challenges in SEO is keyword research and targeting. Finding the right keywords and phrases to target can be time-consuming and overwhelming, especially for those new to SEO. The challenge lies in identifying keywords that are relevant to your website and have a high search volume, but are not too competitive. Additionally, it's important to understand the nuances of keyword targeting, such as long-tail keywords and local keywords, in order to effectively target the right audience. To overcome this challenge, beginners should start by researching keywords related to their niche and focus on long-tail keywords with lower competition.

Another major challenge in SEO is competition. There are millions of websites out there, and many of them are competing for the same keywords and search engine rankings. It can be difficult to stand out among all the noise, particularly for new websites with limited resources. The key to overcoming this challenge is to understand your competition and create a unique value proposition. This means identifying what makes your website unique and leveraging that uniqueness to stand out from other websites in your niche. For example, a website selling handmade crafts might differentiate itself from competitors by emphasizing its use of sustainable materials or its focus on local artisans.

Website structure and technical SEO is another big challenge in SEO. Issues with website structure, such as broken links, crawl errors, and poor mobile optimization, can negatively impact search engine rankings and drive away potential visitors. It's crucial to have a website that is easy to navigate and optimized for both search engines and users. This means paying attention to details such as site structure, URL structure, and meta descriptions, as well as ensuring that the website is mobile-friendly and has fast loading times. To overcome this challenge, beginners should start by performing a technical SEO audit of their website and fixing any issues that are identified.

Finally, keeping up with search engine algorithms is a continuous challenge in SEO. Search engines regularly update their algorithms, and it can be difficult to keep up with these changes and adjust SEO strategies accordingly. This is especially true for beginners, who may not have the experience or resources to stay up-to-date with the latest developments in SEO. To overcome this challenge, beginners should regularly read industry blogs and attend SEO conferences and events to stay informed about the latest trends and best practices in SEO.

In conclusion, SEO presents a number of challenges, but with the right approach and determination, they can be overcome. Keyword research and targeting, competition, website structure and technical SEO, and keeping up with search engine algorithms are just some of the key challenges in SEO. By understanding these challenges and developing strategies to overcome them, beginners can achieve high search engine rankings, drive organic traffic to their website, and ultimately succeed in their digital marketing efforts.

Overview of Strategies for Overcoming Key Challenges in SEO

If you're new to search engine optimization (SEO), you may feel overwhelmed by the various challenges that come with optimizing a website for search engines. However, the good news is that there are strategies you can use to overcome these challenges and achieve success in search engine rankings.

Let's take a closer look at some of the key strategies for overcoming common SEO challenges.

Keyword Research and Targeting

One of the biggest challenges in SEO is finding the right keywords and phrases to target. This can be a time-consuming and overwhelming process, especially for beginners. However, there are several strategies you can use to make the process easier and more effective.

The first step is to understand the importance of keywords and how they impact your search engine rankings. You should then conduct thorough keyword research to identify the keywords and phrases that are most relevant to your website and your target audience.

Once you've identified your target keywords, you can use a variety of strategies to target them effectively. This includes creating keyword-optimized content, optimizing your website's meta tags, and using internal and external links with targeted keywords. You should also focus on creating high-quality, relevant, and engaging content that will attract and retain visitors.

Competition

Another major challenge in SEO is competition. With so many websites vying for top search engine rankings, it can be difficult to stand out from the crowd. However, there are several strategies you can use to overcome this challenge.

The first step is to understand your competition. This includes researching their SEO strategies, website structure, and content. You can then develop a unique value proposition that sets your website apart from the rest. This could be a unique product or service, a unique approach to your industry, or a unique approach to content creation and optimization.

In addition, you should focus on creating high-quality, relevant, and engaging content that will attract and retain visitors. You should also work on building high-quality backlinks from authoritative websites. This will help to increase your website's authority and improve your search engine rankings.

Website Structure and Technical SEO

Another major challenge in SEO is website structure and technical SEO. Issues with website structure, such as broken links, crawl errors, and poor mobile optimization, can negatively impact your search engine rankings.

To overcome this challenge, it's important to focus on creating a user-friendly website with a clear and concise structure. This includes using descriptive and accurate titles and meta descriptions, using header tags to structure your content, and using internal and external links to help users navigate your website.

You should also focus on improving your website's technical SEO. This includes ensuring that your website is mobile-friendly, that your website loads quickly, and that you use secure connections (HTTPS). You should also make sure that your website is free of crawl errors, and that you use sitemaps and robots.txt files to help search engines understand your website's structure.

In conclusion, these are just a few of the strategies you can use to overcome the challenges of SEO. Whether you're new to SEO or a seasoned pro, it's important to stay up-to-date with the latest trends and best practices. With a little hard work and dedication, you can achieve top search engine rankings and attract more visitors to your website.

So, don't give up! Stay focused, stay motivated, and don't be afraid to try new things. With the right strategies and a little bit of creativity, you can achieve success in search engine optimization and reach your goals.

Encouragement to Continue Learning and Improving SEO Skills

As you delve deeper into the world of SEO, it's important to remember that this is a constantly evolving field that requires continuous learning and improvement. The more you learn, the better you'll be able to tackle the challenges of search engine optimization and achieve success for your website. Whether you're a beginner or a seasoned pro, there's always room for growth, and the rewards for doing so are substantial.

First and foremost, it's important to have a passion for SEO. Without a genuine love for the field and a desire to learn and grow, it can be easy to become discouraged and lose sight of your goals.
However, if you have a true passion for SEO, you'll find that the challenges you face only serve to fuel your desire to learn more and improve your skills.

One of the biggest benefits of continuous learning in SEO is the ability to stay ahead of the curve. The algorithms used by search engines are constantly changing, and the best practices for optimization are constantly evolving. By staying up-to-date with the latest developments, you'll be better equipped to make informed decisions and stay ahead of the competition.

Additionally, continued learning will help you develop a deeper understanding of the principles of SEO. This knowledge will give you a stronger foundation upon which to build your optimization efforts, and will allow you to make more informed decisions that lead to better results. Whether you're focusing on keyword research, link building, or any other aspect of SEO, the more you know, the more effective you'll be.

Perhaps one of the most important benefits of continuous learning in SEO is the sense of accomplishment it provides. As you learn new skills and apply them to your optimization efforts, you'll begin to see real results, and you'll feel a sense of pride and satisfaction in your accomplishments. Whether it's a higher search engine ranking, more traffic, or improved conversions, the sense of accomplishment you feel will be a powerful motivator that keeps you focused and driven.

So how can you continue to learn and improve your SEO skills? There are many resources available to you, and the best approach is to find the ones that work best for you and stick with them. Some of the most popular resources include:

Books: There are countless books available on SEO, and many of them are geared towards beginners. Whether you're interested in keyword research, link building, or any other aspect of SEO, you're sure to find a book that will help you improve your skills.

Online courses: Online courses offer a flexible and convenient way to learn SEO, and many of them are available for free or at a low cost. From video tutorials to interactive courses, there are many options to choose from.

Blogs and forums: The SEO community is incredibly active, and there are countless blogs and forums dedicated to discussing the latest developments in the field. By participating in these communities, you'll have access to a wealth of information and resources, as well as the opportunity to network with other SEO professionals.

Conferences and events: Attending conferences and events is a great way to stay up-to-date with the latest developments in SEO, and to network with other professionals in the field. From regional events to large-scale conferences, there are many opportunities to choose from.

In conclusion, the key to success in SEO is a love for the field and a desire to learn and grow. By constantly learning and improving your skills, you'll stay ahead of the curve, develop a deeper understanding of the principles of SEO, and feel a sense of accomplishment in your efforts. So don't be afraid to dive in and start exploring the world of SEO!

Final Thoughts

In this book, we covered the three major challenges faced by beginners in the field of search engine optimization: keyword research and targeting, competition, and website structure and technical SEO. We hope that by reading this book, you have gained a better understanding of these challenges and feel more confident in your ability to overcome them.

The world of SEO can be complex and ever-changing, but with the right knowledge and strategies, you can succeed in getting your website to the top of search engine rankings. Remember, SEO is a journey, not a destination. It takes time, effort, and a willingness to learn and adapt to changes in the industry.

The importance of keyword research and targeting cannot be overstated. Without the right keywords, your website will not be seen by the right audience. You need to put in the time and effort to understand what your target audience is searching for and then create content that meets their needs and interests. This will not only increase your visibility in search engine rankings but also improve user experience, which is critical to the success of your website.

Competition in the world of SEO can be fierce, but this should not discourage you. Instead, use it as motivation to stand out from the crowd. Take the time to understand your competition, what sets you apart from them, and what makes your website unique. Leverage your strengths and invest in quality content, user experience, and technical SEO to make your website stand out.

Finally, website structure and technical SEO can greatly impact your search engine rankings. A user-friendly website with good structure and optimal technical SEO will not only improve your search engine visibility but also provide a positive user experience. Make sure to regularly check for broken links, crawl errors, and other technical issues, and invest in the tools and resources needed to improve your website structure and technical SEO.

In conclusion, overcoming the challenges of SEO requires a commitment to continuous learning and improvement. The world of SEO is constantly evolving, and it is important to stay up-to-date with the latest trends and best practices. Don't be afraid to take risks and try new strategies. With persistence and determination, you can achieve success in the world of SEO.

For example, consider a small business owner who has struggled with keyword research and targeting. After reading this book, they are now able to conduct thorough keyword research, understand the needs and interests of their target audience, and create content that meets those needs and interests. They are now seeing increased website traffic and a boost in search engine rankings, and they feel confident in their ability to continue improving their SEO strategies.

Or consider a website owner who was struggling with competition. After reading this book, they understand the importance of developing a unique value proposition and are now able to differentiate themselves from their competition. They are now standing out in search engine rankings and are proud of the hard work and effort they put into their website.

In both examples, the individuals have overcome their SEO challenges and are now seeing success because of their commitment to continuous learning and improvement.

We hope this book has provided you with valuable insights and strategies for overcoming the challenges of SEO. Good luck on your journey and don't forget to keep learning and growing!